I KNOW MY FATHER

AND

AT YOUR COMMAND

Neville Goddard

CLASSY
PUBLISHING

I KNOW MY FATHER AND AT YOUR COMMAND
by Neville Goddard

Published by Classy Publishing, 2023

www.classypublishing.com
info@classypublishing.com

ISBN: 978-93-5522-490-3

No part of this publication may be reproduced, stored in a retrieval system, or transmitted, in any form or by any means, electronic, mechanical, photocopying, recording or otherwise, without the prior permission of the publisher.

Cover Design by Classy Publishing

CONTENTS

I Know My Father		1
I.	I Am	3
II.	I Come with a Sword	6
III.	The Foundation Stone	9
IV.	The I'm-Pression	15
V.	He Who Has	18
VI.	Circumcision	20
VII.	Crucifixion and Resurrection	23
VIII.	No Other God	26
IX.	Thy will be Done	29
X.	Be Ears that Hear	33
At Your Command		37

I KNOW MY FATHER

I

I AM

"My Father is he whom men call God, but I know my Father and men know not their God." My Father and Your Father are One. "Hear, O Israel, the Lord our God is One Lord." "I and my Father are One."

One Father made us all to live, move and have our being in Him the One. Who then is this ONE that we have in common? The one and only thing all men have in common is this, all men know that they are. This claim that we are, this awareness, is our Father.

There is no place that man can go and not know that he is. "If I take the wings of the morning and fly to the uttermost parts of the earth thou art there", I know that I Am.

"If I make my bed in Hell"- I know that I AM. If I should suffer from amnesia and completely forget my human identity I will still know that I AM. It is impossible for man to know that he is not. You can say I AM not that, but you cannot say I AM not, for your very knowing is a declaration that you are.

So whether you claim yourself to be or not to be, you are actually claiming that you are. Thus man is ever saying I AM. This knowing that we are, this awareness, is God the Father. The moment this unconditioned awareness becomes conditioned by claiming itself to be this that or the other, a differentiation takes place within this formless awareness, and our impersonal Father (Our real self) becomes personified as that which we have conceived ourselves to be.

This impersonal presence that we are may be likened to space, for space though formless gives form to all. If the formless space was extracted from the book you are reading, the body you wear, the earth you stand on, all would vanish.

Consciousness though formless, gives form to that which it is conscious of being, but the moment you withdraw your formless reality or consciousness from your conception of yourself (the form you wear) this conception passes away. A conception remains a formed reality only as long as the invisible reality wears it.

"My Father is Spirit (Formless) and they that worship him must worship him in Spirit and in Truth." "I and my Father are one." My awareness of being is the formless Father who gives form to that which I am aware of being, and in so doing loses its formless, nameless presence, in the form and nature of its conception of itself.

As water loses its identity when mixed with things and yet remains untarnished when it is extracted through distillation, so the awareness the no-thing-loses itself in things-conceptions of itself and remains its immaculate self through spiritual distillation. You are spiritually distilled or extracted from your conception of yourself when you cease to be identified with it.

Now that you have found this one to be your Father, the Eternal Now, I AM, do not return to the prodigal state to beg for the crumbs of life. Remember your Father, the NOW, the only reality.

Claim yourself now, this moment, to be that which you desire to be and regardless of what your claim may be your Father, the awareness that is Now, will give it to you by becoming the thing claimed but you must ask him in this manner.

Be aware of being that for which you ask. No longer look for your Father in time and space, For your Father is the awareness that is now. "I and my Father are one, but my Father is greater than I." My awareness and that which I AM Aware of being are one, but I AM greater than that which I AM aware of being. The conceiver will ever be greater than his conception. The Father (Consciousness) is greater than his SON (conception of himself).

Now your eyes are opened. Your Father, God Almighty, has been revealed to you as your awareness of being.

II

I COME WITH A SWORD

Before you can enter into that peace which passeth all understanding, you must first be slain of all the illusions that now enslave you, the illusions of divisions.

If you are identified with race, creed or color and hear that with which you are identified, criticised and condemned, you will be automatically hurt by such criticism. Every attachment is a bar in your self-created prison. Your only escape lies in non-attachment. You must leave all and follow me. In Christ there is neither Greek nor Jew bond nor free.

Your present attachments are rooted in you because of your present conception of yourself. Your conception of yourself is the measuring rod by which you measure the world.

All things are judged in relationship to your present conception of yourself. Every man's conception of himself is a vibrant note in the Cosmic Symphony, which note automatically determines the value of all notes in relationship to itself.

Change your conception of yourself. Revalue yourself and you will automatically change your world. Man has always played the losing game by attempting to change his world, while he himself remained with his present values or conceptions of himself.

Jesus discovered this law. So instead of changing men he changed himself. He said, "And now I sanctify myself, that they also might be sanctified through the truth." He found himself to be the truth of all that he saw his world to be.

Truth is the sword that slays all but itself, and I AM (your awareness) is the truth. Therefore to be identified with anything other than being is to be enslaved, or limited by that with which you are identified.

You eternally objectify that which you are conscious of being, so you forever move in a world that is the perfect personification of that which you know yourself to be.

"To the pure all things are pure." This is a great hurdle to those who are constantly condemning the world. "There is therefore no condemnation to those in Christ Jesus."

It is recorded that the crowds left Jesus when he revealed the working of the law in these words, "No man cometh unto me save the Father in me draw him." And- "I and my Father are one."

They could not believe that they were the cause of all they saw their world to be. After thousands of years it is still the great stumbling block to all who see the world as something to be changed on the outside.

You and your conception of yourself are one. Your conception of yourself is the image you have made of your Father. This image fashions your world in your likeness, be it good bad or indifferent. Your Father is your awareness who limits you to that which you are aware of being. If you would change your world do so in truth, by knowing yourself to be all you see the world to be. You are not what you are because of anything in the world, on the contrary, The world is what it is because of what you are; the WHAT being the measure or value you have placed upon yourself. In short, your conception of yourself is the mould the conceiver (your true Self) uses to people your world. Begin to transform the world by claiming yourself to be that which you desire to see expressed in the world. Follow the example of Jesus who made Himself one with God, and found it not strange or robbery to do the work of God.

Freedom is not won by the sweat of the brow. Stop wrestling with the world, it is only a reflector. Jacob was freed only as he loosed that with which he wrestled. Likewise, you will be free only as you follow his example and loose your problem by not identifying yourself with it. For that which is bound in heaven (Consciousness) is bound on earth and that which is loosed in Heaven is loosed on earth. "You shall know the truth and the truth shall set you free." "I AM the truth." So in reality to know yourself the conditioned, is to be free from that which in your blindness you believed yourself to be. Leave all and just be ME.

III

THE FOUNDATION STONE

"Seek ye the Kingdom of Heaven and all things will be added unto you." Find the cause of things and you have found the secret of creation. You have heard it said, that "In the beginning God created the heaven and the earth", that "all things were made by him; and without him was not anything made that was made." No one questions the truth of this statement, but what one does want to know is- "who is God and where is God located?" In answer to the who you are told, "I AM God, I AM the lord, I AM hath sent me (the man Moses) unto you." As to the location of God you are told, "The Kingdom of God is within you." These two answers identify God as your awareness of being and locates him where you are aware of being. To be conscious of being is to silently declare, "I AM." As you read this page you are aware of being. This awareness, this consciousness of being, is God the creator. Awareness is that formless deep in which all things live, move and have their being, and apart from which things have no reality. This is the secret of the statement, "Before Abraham was, I AM, before the world was, I AM and when all things shall cease to be, I AM."

Awareness of being precedes all conceptions of itself and remains its formless self when all of its conceptions cease to be. The creator must precede creation, as the conceiver precedes his conceptions. Creation begins and ends in the Creator. Consciousness is the secret of all manifestion. Every creation passes through three stages in its unfoldment, conception, crucifixion and resurrection. Ideas, desires, ambitions are all conceptions moving within the motionless being, I AM. Consciousness is Father and all conceptions of itself are children bearing witness of their Father. Therefore, "I and my Father are one, but my Father is greater than I"; the conceiver and the conception are one, but the conceiver is greater than its conception.

Awareness is unconditioned. To be aware of being something or someone is conditioning the unconditioned. That which is defined is less than the definer. Awareness of being is the Almighty God, the Everlasting Father, upon whose shoulders is the government of the world. Awareness sustains and directs all things that it is aware of being. Consciousness of being is the eternal womb impregnating itself through the medium of desire. To be conscious of an urge or desire is to have conceived. To believe, by feeling yourself (The Formless) to be the thing desired, is to be crucified upon the form of the thing felt. To continue in the belief, feeling that you are now the thing desired until all doubts cease and a deep conviction is born that it is so is to be resurrected or visibly lifted into expressing the nature of the thing felt.

At this very moment you are resurrecting or expressing that which you are conscious of being. "I AM the resurrection and the life." I AM now out-picturing in the world round about me, as a living reality, that which I am now aware that I AM-

and I shall continue to do so until I change my conception of myself. So your answer in consciousness to the eternal question, WHO AM I, Will determine your world and its every expression. Begin now to realize that I AM is the Lord God Almighty and beside ME (your awareness) There is no other God. Not I, John Doe is God but I AM, the awareness of being, is God. John Doe is only its present limitation or conception of itself. I am the limitless expressing through the limited conception of myself. To change the expression change the conception of yourself but do so in truth, not in words. That is turn your attention completely away from your present limitation and place it upon the new conception, until the awareness, your true being, is lost in the belief or conviction that I AM that I AM.

This is the reclothing or rebirth of your formless, nameless self. Your true self is a self, who no man sees, and who sees not itself, but sees only its conception of itself. In the beginning, now this moment, the idea or desire is swimming around in your consciousness seeking embodiment. Before the desire can be realized or resurrected, it must first become a cross or fixed point upon which consciousness is nailed. Awareness is the only living reality, the only resurrecting power. So to give life to my desire, I must in consciousness become aware of being the thing desired. "Let there be a firmament in the midst of the waters." In the midst of the waters or formless awareness, let there be a firmness or conviction that I AM the thing desired. Continue to stand upon this conviction or cross, and in ways unknown to you as man, you will realize or resurrect your desire. Life or awareness has ways that man (the conception) Knows not of its ways are past finding out. Life's present conception of itself as man is a mask that it wears. Within this being that you think you are, is your nameless self I AM.

The foundation of all expression is consciousness and other foundations no man can lay. Try as man will he cannot find another cause of manifestation other than God his consciousness of being. Man thinks he has found the cause of disease in germs; the cause of war in conflicting political ideologies and greed. All such discoveries of man, catalogued as they are as the essence of wisdom, are foolishness in the eyes of God. There is only one power and this power is God (Consciousness). It kills, it makes alive, it wounds, it heals, it does all things good, bad or indifferent.

A prisoner must have a jailer, a slave a master. A nation that feels itself to be imprisoned will automatically create a dictator. You could no more rub out a tyrant by destroying him, than you can your reflection by destroying the mirror. The consciousness of a nation produces its leaders. That which is true of a nation is true of an individual, for nations are made up of individuals. Man moves in a world that is nothing more nor less than his consciousness objectified. Not knowing this, he wars against his reflections while he keeps alive the light and the images which throw the reflections. "I AM the light of the world." I AM (consciousness is the light.) That which I am conscious of being (my conception of myself) such as, I am rich, I am healthy, I am free-are the images.

The world is the mirror magnifying all that I AM conscious of being. Stop trying to change the world, it is only a mirror telling you who you are.

The man who is conscious of being free or imprisoned is expressing that which he is conscious of being. I do not care what men have diagnosed your problem to be. A problem might have a history ages long, yet I know it will vanish in the twinkle of an eye, if you will faithfully follow this instruction.

Ask yourself this simple question. How would I feel if I were free? The very moment you sincerely ask this question the answer comes.

No man can tell another how that other would feel if his desire were suddenly realized. But everyone would know how he himself would feel, for such feeling would be automatic.

The feeling or thrill that comes to one in response to his self-questioning is the Father state of consciousness or Foundation Stone, from which will come the thing felt. Just how this feeling will embody itself no one knows but it will for the Father (consciousness) has ways that no man knows of.

Make the new feeling natural by wearing it. All things express their nature, so you must wear this feeling until it becomes your nature. It might take a moment or a year it is entirely up to you. The moment all doubts vanish and you feel I AM this, you begin to bear the fruit of the nature of the thing you are feeling yourself to be. When a person buys a new hat or pair of shoes he thinks everyone knows that they are new. He feels unnatural with them on until he wears them long enough to make them natural. The same applies to the wearing of the new state of consciousness.

When you ask yourself the question, "How would I feel if my desire were this moment realized?" -the automatic reply is so new that you Feel that it is not yours, that it is not true. Therefore, you instantly put this new state of consciousness off and immediately return to your problem because it is more natural. Not knowing that consciousness is ever out-picturing itself in conditions round about you- You, like Lot's wife, look back upon your problem and once again become hypnotized by its naturalness. Do you not hear the words of Jesus (salvation)? "Leave all and follow me- let the dead bury their dead." Your problem might have you so hypnotized by its seeming reality and naturalness, that you find it difficult to wear the new feeling, or consciousness of your saviour but wear it you must if you would have results. The stone (Consciousness) which the builders rejected (would not wear) is the chief corner Stone and other foundations no man can lay.

IV

THE I'M-PRESSION

Every impression must become the affirmation of that which is to be. To say that I shall be great or that I shall be free is a confession that I am not great and I Am not free. To see yourself as becoming anything is to know that I am not that thing. To be Impressed- is to be I'm-pressed-first person, present tense. All expressions are the result of I'm-pressions. Only as I can claim myself to be that which I desire to be will I express such claims. Let all your desires be impressions of that which is, not that which is to be. For I'm (your awareness) is God, and God is the fullness of all, the Eternal NOW-I AM-I'm.

Signs follow, they do not precede. You will never see the signs of that which is. Take no thought of tomorrow, for your tomorrows are the expressions of your todays impressions. "Now is the accepted time. The Kingdom of Heaven is at hand." Jesus (salvation) said, "I am with you always." Your awareness is the savior that is with you always. But, if you deny him, he will deny you also. You deny him by claiming that he will appear, as millons today are doing when they claim that salvation is to come, which claim is the equivalent of saying,

"We are not saved." You must stop looking for your savior to appear and claim yourself to be saved now, and the signs of your claims shall follow.

When the widow was asked, "what had she in her house," there was recognition of substance, Now, in her claim of three drops of oil, not empty measures. Three drops become a gusher if claimed. For your awareness magnifies all that it is conscious of being. To claim that I shall have oil (Joy) is to confess that I have empty measures, which consciousness of lack, will produce lack. God, your awareness, is no respecter of persons and can only express that with which it is impressed. Your every desire is determined by your need. Desires are automatic. Knowing that you are aware of the desire and that your awareness is God, You should look upon each desire as the spoken words of God, telling you of that which is. "Turn from the seeing of man whose breath is in his nostrils." For he sees his desire as that which is not. We shall ever be that which we are (aware)- so never again claim, I shall be that. Let all claims from now on be-"I AM that I AM."

"Before they ask I have answered." Before you have time to think, the solution of your problem was given you in the form of your desire. The blind, the lame, the halt, all automatically desire freedom from limitation. Man is so schooled in the belief that his desires are things to struggle over, that he in his ignorance, denies his savior who is constantly knocking at the door of consciousness (I AM the Door) to be let in. Would not your desire, if realized, save you from your problem? To let your savior in is the easiest thing in the world. Things must be, to be let in. You are conscious of a desire, therefore, the desire is something that you are aware of now. Your desire, though invisible, must be affirmed by you to be something that is real. "God calleth those things which be not (are not seen) as though they were." The claim I AM He (the thing desired) is letting your savior in.

Every desire is the savior's knock at the door. This knock, every man hears. Man opens the door for him to enter when he claims- I AM He. See to it that you let your savior in, by letting the thing desired press itself upon you, until you are I'mpressed with the Nowness of your savior, and utter the cry of Victory, "It is finished."

V

HE WHO HAS

"For he that hath, To him shall be given and To he that hath not, from him shall be taken even that which he hath." Though many look upon this statement to be the most cruel and unjust of the sayings attributed to Jesus- creating as it has the world over the many popular remarks, such as, the rich get richer and the poor get children; he who has gets, etc.,-it still remains a most just and merciful law based upon a changeless principle.

God is no respecter of persons. God, as we have discovered, is that unconditioned awareness who gives to each and all, that which they are aware of being. To be aware of being or having anything is to be or have that which you are aware of being. Upon this changeless principle all things rest. It is impossible for anything to be other than that which it is aware of being. "To him that hath (That which he is aware of Being) It shall be given"- good, bad or indifferent. It does not matter what it is that you are aware of being, you will receive pressed down, shaken together and running over, all that you are conscious of being. In keeping with this same changeless law, "To Him that hath not, It shall be taken from and added to the one that hath." So the rich do get richer and the poor get poorer. Yes, He who has Gets.

You cannot express that which you are not conscious of being. You cannot serve two masters. Your master is ever that state of consciousness with which you are identified. Therefore that which is not in consciousness is taken from it- (because it was never part of it) and added to that consciousness which it is aware of it. All things gravitate to that consciousness with which they are in tune, and likewise, all things disentangle themselves from that consciousness with which they are not in tune. So instead of joining the chorus of the have nots who insist on destroying those who have, recognize this changeless law of expression and consciously claim yourself to be that which you have decided to be. After your decision is made and your conscious claim established, continue in your confidence until you receive your reward. For as the day follows the night, you will receive that which you have consciously claimed for yourself.

Thus, that which to the sleeping orthodox world is a cruel and unjust law, becomes to the enlightened, the most merciful and just statement of truth. "I am come not to destroy but to fulfill."

Knowing that God does not destroy anything, see to it that you are that, claim yourself to be that which you want him to fill-full. Nothing is destroyed. All are fulfilled.

VI

CIRCUMCISION

Circumcision is the operation which removes the veil that hides the head of creation. The physical act has nothing to do with the spiritual act.

The whole world could be physically circumcised and yet remain unclean and blind leaders of the blind. The spiritually circumcised have had the veil of darkness removed and know themselves to be Christ, the light of the World.

Let me now perform the spiritual operation on you, the reader. This act is performed on the eighth day after birth; eight, because eight is the figure that has neither beginning nor ending. Furthermore, the ancients symbolized the eighth numeral as an enclosure or veil, within and behind which lay buried the mystery of creation. Thus, the secret of the operation on the eighth day is in keeping with the nature of the act, which act, is to reveal the eternal head of creation; that changeless something in which all things begin and end, and remains its eternal self when all things cease to be. This mysterious something is your awareness of being. At this moment you are aware of being, but you are aware of being someone. This someone is the veil that hides the being that you really are. You are first conscious of being, then you are conscious of being man. After the veil of man is placed upon your faceless self you become conscious of being a member of a certain race, nation, family, creed, etc. The veil to be lifted in spiritual circumcision is the veil of man, but before this can be done, you must cut away the adhesions of race, nation, family and so on.

"In Christ there is neither Greek nor Jew, bond nor free, male nor female." You must leave father, mother, brother and follow me. To accomplish this you must stop identifying yourself with these divisions, by becoming indifferent to such claims. Indifference is the knife that severs. Feeling is the tie that binds. When you can look upon man as one grand brotherhood without distinction of race, creed or color, then you will know that you have severed these adhesions. With these ties cut all that now separates you from your true being is your belief that you are man.

To remove this last veil, you must drop your conception of yourself as man, by knowing yourself just to be. Instead of the consciousness of -I AM Man, let there be just-I AM- Faceless, Formless Awareness. Then, unveiled and awake you will declare and know that-I AM is God and beside me, this awareness, there is no God. This mystery is told in the bible story of Jesus washing the feet of his disciples. It is recorded that Jesus laid aside his garments and took a towel and girded himself. Then after washing his disciples' feet he wiped them with the towel wherewith he was girded. Peter protested and was told that unless his feet where washed, he would have no part of Jesus. Peter replied, "Lord, not my feet only, but also my hands and head." Jesus answered and said, "He that is washed needeth not save to wash feet, but is clean every whit."

Common sense would tell the reader that a man is not clean all over just because his feet are washed. So he should either discard this story or look for its hidden meaning. Every story of the Bible is a psychological drama taking place in the consciousness of man and this is no exception.

This washing of the disciples' feet is the mystical story of spiritual circumcision or the revealing of the secrets of the lord.

Jesus is called the lord. You are told that the Lord's name is I AM-Je Suis. "I am the lord that is my name." - Isaiah 42:8. Jesus is girded with a towel, therefore his secrets are hidden. Jesus or Lord symbolizes your awareness of being, whose secrets are hidden by the towel- (consiousness of man). The foot symbolizes the understanding (Walk ye in his footsteps- understanding) which must be washed by the lord-awareness- of all human beliefs or conceptions of itself. As the towel is removed to dry the feet the secrets of the Lord are revealed.

In short, the removing of the belief that you are man reveals your awareness as the head of creation. Man is the foreskin hiding the head of creation. I AM the lord hidden by the veil of man.

VII

CRUCIFIXION AND RESURRECTION

The events of crucifixion and resurrection are so interwoven they must be explained together for one determines the other. This mystery is symbolized on earth in the rituals of Good Friday and Easter. You have observed that these days are not fixed but change from year to year. They fall anywhere from the last week of March to the last week of April. The day is determined in this manner. The first Sunday after the full moon in Aries is celebrated as Easter. Aries begins on the 21st day of March and marks the beginning of Spring. This movable date should tell the observant one to look for some interpretation, other than the one given him.

Seen from the earth, the Sun in its northern passage appears at the Spring season of the year to cross the imaginary lineman calls the equator. So it is said, by the mystic, to be crossified or crucified that man might live. They noticed that soon after this event took place, all nature began to rise or resurrect itself from its long winter's sleep, therefore they concluded that this disturbance of nature at this season of the year was due directly to this crossing. Thus they believed that the Son must have shed his blood at the passover. If these dates marked the death and resurrection of Jesus they would be fixed like all other historical events, but this is not the case. However these dates do symbolize the death and resurrection of the lord, but this lord is your awareness of being. It is recorded that he gave His life that you may live- "I AM come that you might have life and that you might have it more abundantly."

As Spring is the time of the year when the millons of seeds, which all winter lay buried in the ground, suddenly spring into visibility that man might live and because the mystical drama of the crucifixion and resurrection is in the nature of this yearly change, it is celebrated at this Spring season of the year but actually it is taking place every moment of time. The being that is crucified is our awareness of being. The cross is your conception of yourself. The resurrection is the lifting into visibility of this conception of yourself. Far from being a day of mourning Good Friday should be a day of rejoicing, for there can be no resurrection without a crucifixion. The thing to be resurrected in your case is that which you desire to be. To do this, you must feel yourself to be the thing desired. You must feel I AM that, for I AM the resurrection and the life. Yes, I AM (Your awareness of being) is the power resurrecting and making alive that which you are aware of being.

Two shall agree on touching anything and I shall establish it on earth. The two agreeing are You (your awareness) and the thing desired (that which you have decided on to be, through becoming aware of it). When this agreement is attained, the crucifixion is completed. Two have crossed or crossified each other. I AM and that (the thing desired) have joined. I AM now nailed upon the form of that.

The nail that binds you upon the cross is the nail of feeling. The mystical marriage is now consummated and the result will be the birth of a child or the resurrection of a son bearing witness of his Father.

Consciousness is wedded to that which it is conscious of being. The world of expression is the child confirming this union. The day you cease to be conscious of being that which you are now conscious of being, that day your child or expression shall die and return to the bosom of his father, the faceless, formless awareness. All expressions are the results of such mystical marriages. So the priests are correct when they say, all true marriages are made in Heaven and can only be dissolved in Heaven. But let me clarify this statement by telling you that Heaven is not a locality, it is a state of consciousness. The Kingdom of Heaven is within you. In Heaven (consciousness) God is touched by that which he is aware of being. "Who has touched Me? For I perceive virtue has gone out of me. " The moment this touching (feeling) takes place, there is an off-springing or going-out-of-me into visibility, taking place.

The day man feels I AM free, I AM wealthy, I AM strong, God (I AM) is touched by these qualities or virtues, and the results of such touching will be seen in the birth or resurrection of the qualities felt. For man must have visible confirmation of all that he is conscious of being. Now you will know why man or manifestation is always made in the image of God.

Your awareness images and out-pictures all that you are aware of being. "I AM the Lord and beside Me there is no other God." I AM the resurrection and the Life!

VIII

NO OTHER GOD

"Thou shalt have no other God beside me." As long as man entertains the belief in powers apart from himself, so long will he rob himself of the being that he is. Every belief in powers apart from yourself, whether for good or evil, will become the moulds of the graven images you will worship.

The belief in the potency of drugs to heal, diets to strengthen, monies to secure, are the values or money changers that must be thrown out of the Temple. "Ye are the Temple of the living God"- a Temple made without hands.

It is written, "My house shall be called of all nations a house of prayer, but ye have made it a den of thieves."

Your beliefs in the potency of things are the thieves that rob you. There is only one power, one Savior-I AM He. It is your belief in the thing and not the thing itself that aids you. Therefore, stop transferring the power that you are to things round about you. Claim yourself to be the power which you have in your ignorance given to another.

It is easier for a camel, burdened as he is with the so-called treasures of life, to go through the needle's eye (a small gate in the walls of Jerusalem, so named because of its narrowness) than a rich man (the opinionated man filled with his human values) to enter the Kingdom of Heaven. Man is so filled with human values (riches) as to the reason of things, that he cannot, through so dark a veil as the wisdom of man, see that the only reason or value to anything is that all things are expressing perfectly that which they are conscious of being. When man realizes that the consciousness of a quality expresses that quality without the aid of anything else, he will become the poor man, the foolish man, who has no reason for anything happening other than that which is happening, is perfectly expressing that which it is conscious of being. Such a one has thrown out the money changers or many values and has now established one value: consciousness.

The Lord is in his holy temple. Consciousness dwells within that which it is conscious of being. I AM man-is the Lord and his Temple. Knowing that the consciousness of wealth produces wealth, as the consciousness of poverty produces poverty, He forgives all men for being what they are. For all are expressing (without the aid of another) that which they are conscious of being. He knows that a change of consciousness will produce a change of expression, so instead of sympathizing with the beggars of life at the temple gate, he declares, "Silver and gold have I none (for thee) but such as I have (the consciousness of freedom) give I unto thee." Stir up the gift within you. Stop begging, and claim yourself to be that which you were begging for. Do this and you too will jump from your crippled world into the world of freedom, singing praises to the lord, I AM.

"Far greater is he that is in you, than he that is in the world." This cry of everyone who finds His awareness of being to be God.

Your recognition of this fact will automatically cleanse the temple of the thieves and robbers and restore to you that dominion over things which you lost the moment you forgot the command, "Thou shalt have no other God beside me!"

IX

THY WILL BE DONE

"Not my will, but thine be done." This resignation is not one of blind fatalism but it is the illumined realization that, "I can of myself do nothing, the Father within me he doeth the work." When man wills he attempts to make something appear in time and space which he knows does not now exist. He is not aware of what it is he is really doing. But, what he actually does is this. He consciously states, I do not possess the capacities to express it now, but I will acquire these capacities in time. In short-I AM not, but I will be.

Man does not realize that consciousness is the Father who does the work, so he attempts to express that which he is not conscious of being. Such struggles are doomed to disappointment, for only the present expresses itself. Unless I am conscious of being that which I seek, I will not find it. God (your awareness) is the substance and fullness of all. God's will is the recognition of that which is, not of that which shall be. Instead of seeing this saying as, "Thy, will be done"- see it as, "Thy will, be done" (is done). The works are finished. The principle by which all things are made visible is eternal. Even though, "Eyes have not seen nor ears heard, neither hath it entered into the hearts of man, the things which God hath prepared for those who love the law."

When a sculptor looks at a formless piece of marble he sees buried within its formless self, his finished piece of art. So the sculptor instead of making his masterpiece, merely reveals it, by removing that part of the marble which hides his conception.

The same applies to you. In your formless awareness- I AM- lies buried all that you will ever conceive yourself to be. The recognition of this truth will transform you from that of an unskilled laborer, who tries to make it so, to that of a great artist, who recognizes it to be so.

Your claim that you are now that which you want to be, will remove the veil of human darkness with its-I will be-and reveal your perfect claim-I AM that.

God's will was expressed in the words of the widow, "It is well." Man's will would have been, "It shall be well." To state I shall be well is to say, "I AM ill." God, the Eternal now, is not mocked by words or vain repetition. God continually personifies that which is.

Thus, the resignation of Jesus (who made himself Equal with God) was turning from the recognition of lack (which the future indicates with I shall be) to the recognition of supply by claiming- I AM that.

Now you will see the wisdom in the words of the prophet when he stated, "Let the weak say, I AM Strong." - Joel 3:10. Man in his blindness will not heed the prophet's advice, so, he continues to claim himself to be weak, poor wretched and all the other undesirable expressions from which he is trying to free himself, by ignorantly claiming that he will be free from them.

There is only one door through which That Which You Seek can enter your world. When you say, I AM, you are declaring yourself to be first person, present tense. Again, to know that I AM, is to be conscious of being consciousness is the only door. Therefore, unless you are conscious of being That Which You Seek, you seek in vain. If you judge after appearances you will continue to be enslaved by the evidence of your senses. To break from this hypnotic spell of the senses you are told, "go within and shut the door." The door of the senses must be tightly shut before your new claim can be honored. This closing the door of the senses is not as difficult as it at first appears to be. It is done without effort. It is impossible to serve two masters at the same time. The Masterman serves in that which he is conscious of being. I am Lord and Master of that which I am conscious of being.

It is no effort for me to conjure poverty if I AM conscious of being poor. My servant poverty is compelled to follow me (Consciousness of Poverty) as long as I AM (The Lord) conscious of being poor. Instead of fighting against the evidence of the senses, you simply claim yourself to be that which you desire to be. As your attention is placed on this claim, the door of the senses, automatically close against your former master- that which you were conscious of being. As you become lost in the feeling of being this which you are now claiming yourself to be true of yourself, the doors once more open (but as you have discovered, they permit only the present that which I

AM now conscious of being-to enter) and you behold your world expressing that which you are conscious of being. Therefore let us follow the example of Jesus, who, realizing that he could as man do nothing to change his present picture of lack closed the door of his senses and went to his Father, to whom all things are possible. Having denied the evidence of his senses, he claimed himself to be that which but a moment before his senses told him that he was not. Knowing that consciousness expresses its likeness on earth, he remained in the claimed consciousness until the doors (his senses) opened and confirmed the Rulership of the Lord. Remember, I AM is Lord of all. Never again use the will of man which claims I will be. Be as resigned as Jesus, and claim- I AM that.

X

BE EARS THAT HEAR

"Let these sayings sink down in your ears, for the Son of Man shall be delivered into the hands of man." Be not as those who have eyes and see not, and ears and hear not. Let these l revelations sink deep into your ears. For after the son (idea) is made manifest, man with his false values (reason) will attempt to explain the why and wherefore of the son's expression, and in so doing will rend him to pieces. After men have agreed that a certain thing is impossible to do, let someone accomplish the impossible thing–and all, including the wise ones who said it could not be done– will begin to tell you why it happened. After they are all through tearing the seamless robe (cause of manifestation) apart, they will be as far from the truth as they were when they proclaimed it impossible.

As long as man looks for the cause of expression in places other than the expressor, he looks in vain. For thousands of years man has been told, "I AM the life and light of the world." "No manifestation cometh unto me save I draw it."

But man will not believe it, he prefers to believe in causes outside of himself. The moment that which was not seen becomes seen, man is ready to explain the cause and purpose of its appearance. Thus the Son of Man (ideas of manifestation) is constantly being destroyed by the hands (reasonable explanation or wisdom) of man. Now that your awareness is revealed to you as cause of all expression, do not return to the darkness of Egypt with its many Gods. There is but one God. The one God is your awareness. "And all the inhabitants of the earth are reputed as nothing. And he doeth according to his will in the army of heaven, and among the inhabitants of the earth and none can stay his hand, or say unto him, what doest thou?" If the whole world should agree that a thing could not be done, and you became aware of being that which they had agreed upon could not be expressed–you would express it. Your awareness never asks permission to express that which you are aware of being. It does so naturally and without effort in spite of the wisdom of man and the opposition of the armies of both heaven and earth.

"Salute no man by the way", is not a command to be insolent or unfriendly, but a reminder not to recognize a superior, nor to see in anyone a barrier to your expression. For none can stay your hand or question your ability to express that which you are conscious of being. Do not judge after the appearances of a thing, for all are as nothing in the eyes of God. When the disciples, through their judgment of appearances, saw the insane child, they thought it a more difficult problem to solve than others they had seen–and so failed to achieve a cure. In judging after appearances they forgot that all things were possible to God. Hypnotized as they were to the reality of appearances they could not feel the naturalness of sanity. The only way for you to avoid such failures is to constantly bear in mind that your awareness is the Almighty, all-wise presence, who without help, effortlessly out-pictures that which you are aware of being. Be perfectly indifferent to the evidence of the senses, so that you may feel the naturalness of your desire–and your desire will be realized. Turn from appearances and feel the naturalness of perfect sanity and sanity will embody itself. Your desire is the solution of your problem. As the desire is realized, the problem is dissolved. Your desires are the invisible realities which respond only to the commands of God. God commands the invisible to appear by claiming himself to be the thing commanded. "He made himself equal with God and found it not robbery to do the works of God." Now, "let this saying sink deep in your ear" – BE CONSCIOUS OF BEING THAT WHICH YOU WANT TO APPEAR.

AT YOUR COMMAND

LETTER FROM NEVILLE

This book contains the very essence of the Principle of Expression. Had I cared to, I could have expanded it into a book of several hundred pages, but such expansion would have defeated the purpose of this book.

Commands, to be effective, must be short and to the point. The greatest command ever recorded is found in the few simple words: "And God said, 'Let there be light.'"

In keeping with this principle, I now give to you the reader, in these few pages, the truth as it was revealed to me.

—Neville

I

Can man decree a thing and have it come to pass? Most decidedly he can! Man has always decreed that which has appeared in his world and is today decreeing that which is appearing in his world and shall continue to do so as long as man is conscious of being man. Not one thing has ever appeared in man's world but what man decreed that it should. This you may deny, but try as you will you cannot disprove it, for this decreeing is based upon a changeless principle.

You do not command things to appear by your words or loud affirmations. Such vain repetition is more often than not confirmation of the opposite. Decreeing is ever done in consciousness. That is, every man is conscious of being that which he has decreed himself to be. The dumb man without using words is conscious of being dumb. Therefore he is decreeing himself to be dumb.

When the Bible is read in this light you will find it to be the greatest scientific book ever written. Instead of looking upon the Bible as the historical record of an ancient civilization or the biography of the unusual life of Jesus, see it as a great psychological drama taking place in the consciousness of man.

Claim it as your own and you will suddenly transform your world from the barren deserts of Egypt to the promised land of Canaan.

Everyone will agree with the statement that all things were made by God, and without him there is nothing made that is made, but what man does not agree upon is the identity of God. All the churches and priesthoods of the world disagree as to the identity and true nature of God. The Bible proves beyond the shadow of a doubt that Moses and the prophets were in one hundred per cent accord as to the identity and nature of God. And Jesus' life and teachings are in agreement with the findings of the prophets of old.

Moses discovered God to be man's awareness of being, when he declared these little understood words, "I AM hath sent me unto you." David sang in his psalms, "Be still and know that I AM God." Isaiah declared, "I AM the Lord and there is none else. There is no God beside me. I girded thee, though thou hast not known me. I form the light, and create darkness; I make peace, and create evil. I the Lord do all these things."

The awareness of being as God is stated hundreds of times in the New Testament. To name but a few: "I AM the shepherd, I AM the door; I AM the resurrection and the life; I AM the way; I AM the Alpha and Omega; I AM the beginning and the end"; and again, "Whom do you say that I AM?"

It is not stated, "I, Jesus, am the door. I, Jesus am the way," nor is it said, "Whom do you say that I, Jesus, am?". It is clearly stated, "I AM the way." The awareness of being is the door through which the manifestations of life pass into the world of form.

Consciousness is the resurrecting power – resurrecting that which man is conscious of being. Man is ever out-picturing that which he is conscious of being. This is the truth that makes man free, for man is always self-imprisoned or self-freed.

If you, the reader, will give up all of your former beliefs in a God apart from yourself, and claim God as your awareness of being – as Jesus and the prophets did – you will transform your world with the realization that, "I and my father are one." This statement, "I and my father are one, but my father is greater than I," seems very confusing; but if interpreted in the light of what we have just said concerning the identity of God, you will find it very revealing.

Consciousness, being God, is as 'father.' The thing that you are conscious of being is the 'son' bearing witness of his 'father.' It is like the conceiver and its conceptions. The conceiver is ever greater than his conceptions yet ever remains one with his conception. For instance, before you are conscious of being man, you are first conscious of being. Then you become conscious of being man. Yet you remain as conceiver, greater than your conception – man.

Jesus discovered this glorious truth and declared himself to be one with God – not a God that man had fashioned. For he never recognized such a God. He said, "If any man should ever come, saying, 'Look here or look there,' believe them not, for the kingdom of God is within you." Heaven is within you. Therefore, when it is recorded that "He went unto his father," it is telling you that he rose in consciousness to the point where he was just conscious of being, thus transcending the limitations of his present conception of himself, called 'Jesus.'

In the awareness of being all things are possible, he said, "You shall decree a thing and it shall come to pass." This is his decreeing – rising in consciousness to the naturalness of being the thing desired. As he expressed it, "And I, if I be lifted up, I shall draw all men unto me." If I be lifted up in consciousness to the naturalness of the thing desired I will draw the manifestation of that desire unto me. For he states, "No man comes unto me save the father within me draws him, and I and my father are one." Therefore, consciousness is the father that is drawing the manifestations of life unto you. You are at this very moment drawing into your world that which you are now conscious of being. Now you can see what is meant by, "You must be born again." If you are dissatisfied with your present expression in life, the only way to change it is to take your attention away form that which seems so real to you and rise in consciousness to that which you desire to be. You cannot serve two masters, therefore to take your attention from one state of consciousness and place it upon another is to die to one and live to the other. The question, "Whom do you say that I AM?" is not addressed to a man called 'Peter' by one called 'Jesus.' This is the eternal question addressed to one's self by one's true being. In other words, "Whom do you say that you are?". For your conviction of yourself — your opinion of yourself — will determine your expression in life.

He states, "You believe in God – believe also in me." In other words, it is the me within you that is this God. Praying then, is seen to be recognizing yourself to be that which you now desire, rather than its accepting form of petitioning a God that does not exist for that which you now desire. So can't you see why the millions of prayers are not answered? Men pray to a God that does not exist. For instance: To be conscious of being poor and to pray to a God for riches is to be rewarded with that which you are conscious of being – which is poverty.

Prayers to be successful must be claiming rather than begging. So if you would pray for riches, turn from your picture of poverty by denying the very evidence of your senses and assume the nature of being wealthy. We are told, "When you pray go within in secret and shut the door. And that which your father sees in secret, with that will he reward you openly."

We have identified the 'father' to be the awareness of being. We have also identified the 'door' to be the awareness of being. So 'shutting the door' is shutting out that which I am now aware of being and claiming myself to be that which I desire to be. The very moment my claim is established to the point of conviction, that moment I begin to draw unto myself the evidence of my claim.

Do not question the how of these things appearing, for no man knows that way. That is, no manifestation knows how the things desired will appear. Consciousness is the way or door through which things appear. He said, "I AM the way" – not 'I,' John Smith, am the way, but "I AM", the awareness of being, is the way through which the thing shall come. The signs always follow. They never precede. Things have no reality other than in consciousness. Therefore, get the consciousness first and the thing is compelled to appear.

You are told, "Seek ye first the kingdom of Heaven and all things shall be added unto you." Get first the consciousness of the things that you are seeking and leave the things alone. This is what is meant by "Ye shall decree a thing and it shall come to pass."

Apply this principle and you will know what it is to "prove me and see." The story of Mary is the story of every man. Mary was not a woman – giving birth in some miraculous way to one called 'Jesus.'

Mary is the awareness of being that ever remains virgin, no matter how many desires it gives birth to. Right now look upon yourself as this virgin Mary – being impregnated by yourself through the medium of desire – becoming one with your desire to the point of embodying or giving birth to your desire.

For instance: It is said of Mary (whom you now know to be yourself) that she knew not a man. Yet she conceived. That is, you, John Smith, have no reason to believe that that which you now desire is possible, but having discovered your awareness of being to be God, you make this awareness your husband and conceive a man child (manifestation) of the Lord. "For thy maker is thine husband; the Lord of hosts is his name; the Lord God of the whole earth shall he be called." Your ideal or ambition is this conception – the first command to her, which is now to yourself, is "Go, tell no man." That is, do not discuss your ambitions or desires with another for the other will only echo your present fears.

Secrecy is the first law to be observed in realizing your desire. The second, as we are told in the story of Mary, is to "Magnify the Lord." We have identified the Lord as your awareness of being. Therefore, to "Magnify the Lord" is to revalue or expand one's present conception of one's self to the point where this revaluation becomes natural. When this naturalness is attained you give birth by becoming that which you are one with in consciousness.

II

The story of creation is given us in digest form in the first chapter of John.

"In the beginning was the word." Now, this very second, is the 'beginning' spoken of. It is the beginning of an urge – a desire. 'The word' is the desire swimming around in your consciousness, seeking embodiment. The urge of itself has no reality; for, "I AM" or the awareness of being is the only reality. Things live only as long as I AM aware of being them; so to realize one's desire, the second line of this first verse of John must be applied. That is, "And the word was with God."

The word, or desire, must be fixed or united with consciousness to give it reality. The awareness becomes aware of being the thing desired, thereby nailing itself upon the form or conception – and giving life unto its conception – or resurrecting that which was heretofore a dead or unfulfilled desire. "Two shall agree as touching anything and it shall be established on earth."

This agreement is never made between two persons. It is between the awareness and the thing desired.

You are now conscious of being, so you are actually saying to yourself, without using words, "I AM." Now, if it is a state of health that you are desirous of attaining, before you have any evidence of health in your world, you begin to FEEL yourself to be healthy. And the very second the feeling "I AM healthy" is attained the two have agreed. That is, I AM and health have agreed to be one and this agreement ever results in the birth of a child which is the thing agreed upon – in this case, health. And because I made the agreement, I express the thing agreed.

So you can see why Moses stated, "I AM hath sent me." For what being, other than I AM could send you into expression? None – for "I AM the way – Beside me there is no other." If you take the wings of the morning and fly into the uttermost parts of the world, or if you make your bed in Hell, you will still be aware of being. You are ever sent into expression by your awareness, and your expression is ever that which you are aware of being.

Again, Moses stated, "I AM that I AM." Now here is something to always bear in mind. You cannot put new wine in old bottles or new patches upon old garments. That is, you cannot take with you into the new consciousness any part of the old man. All of your present beliefs, fears, and limitations are weights that bind you to your present level of consciousness. If you would transcend this level you must leave behind all that is now your present self, or conception of yourself. To do this you take your attention away from all that is now your problem or limitation and dwell upon just being. That is, you say silently but feeling to yourself, "I AM."

Do not condition this 'awareness' as yet. Just declare yourself to be, and continue to do so until you are lost in the feeling of just being – faceless and formless. When this expansion of consciousness is attained, then within this formless deep of yourself, give form to the new conception by FEELING yourself to be THAT which you desire to be. You will find within this deep of yourself all things to be divinely possible. Everything in the world which you can conceive of being is to you —within this present formless awareness — a most natural attainment.

The invitation given us in the Scriptures is "to be absent from the body and be present with the Lord." The 'body' being your former conception of yourself and 'the Lord' your awareness of being. This is what is meant when Jesus said to Nicodemus, "Ye must be born again for except ye be born again ye cannot enter the kingdom of Heaven." That is, except you leave behind you your present conception of yourself and assume the nature of the new birth, you will continue to out-picture your present limitations.

The only way to change your expressions of life is to change your consciousness. For consciousness is the reality that eternally solidifies itself in the things round about you. Man's world in its every detail is his consciousness out-pictured. You can no more change your environment or world by destroying things than you can your reflection by destroying the mirror. Your environment and all within it reflects that which you are in consciousness. As long as you continue to be that in consciousness so long will you continue to out-picture it in your world.

Knowing this, begin to revalue yourself. Man has placed too little value upon himself.

In the Book of Numbers you will read, "In that day there were giants in the land; and we were in our own sight as grasshoppers. And we were in their sight as grasshoppers." This does not mean a time in the dim past when man had the stature of giants. Today is the day, the eternal now when conditions round about you have attained the appearance of giants — such as unemployed, the armies of your enemy, your problems and all things that seem to threaten you; those are the giants that make you feel yourself to be a grasshopper. But, you are told, you were first in your own sight a grasshopper, and because of this, you were to the giants a grasshopper. In other words, you can only be to others what you are first to yourself.

Therefore, to revalue yourself and begin to feel yourself to be the giant, a center of power, is to dwarf these former giants and make of them grasshoppers. "All the inhabitants of the earth are as nothing, and he doeth according to his will in the armies of Heaven and among all the inhabitants of the earth; and none can stay his hand, nor say unto him, 'What doest thou'?" This being spoken of is not the orthodox God sitting in space but the one and only God — the everlasting father, your awareness of being. So awake to the power that you are not as man, but as your true self — a faceless, formless awareness; and free yourself from your self imposed prison.

"I am the good shepherd and know my sheep and am known of mine. My sheep hear my voice and I know them and they will follow me." Awareness is the good shepherd. What I am aware of being is the 'sheep' that follow me. So good a 'shepherd' is your awareness that it has never lost one of the 'sheep' that you are aware of being.

I am a voice calling in the wilderness of human confusion for such as I am aware of being, and never shall there comes a time when that which I am convinced that I am shall fail to find me. "I AM" is an open door for all that I am to enter. Your awareness of being is lord and shepherd of your life. So, "The Lord is my shepherd; I shall not want" is seen in its true light now to be your consciousness. You could never be in want of proof or lack the evidence of that which you are aware of being.

This being true, why not become aware of being great, God-loving, wealthy, healthy, and all attributes that you admire?

It is just as easy to possess the consciousness of these qualities as it is to possess their opposites, for you have not your present consciousness because of your world. On the contrary, your world is what it is because of your present consciousness. Simple, is it not? Too simple in fact for the wisdom of man that tries to complicate everything.

Paul said of this principle, "It is to the Greeks (or wisdom of this world) foolishness." "And to the Jews (or those who look for signs) a stumbling block", with the result, that man continues to walk in darkness rather than awaken to the being that he is. Man has so long worshipped the images of his own making that at first he finds this revelation blasphemous, since it spells death to all his previous beliefs in a God apart from himself.

This revelation will bring the knowledge that "I and my father are one but my father is greater than I." You are one with your present conception of yourself. But you are greater than that which you are at present aware of being.

Before man can attempt to transform his world he must first lay the foundation: "I AM the Lord." That is, man's awareness, his consciousness of being is God. Until this is firmly established so that no suggestion or argument put forward by others can shake it, he will find himself returning to the slavery of his former beliefs.

"If ye believe not that I AM he, ye shall die in your sins." That is, you shall continue to be confused and thwarted until you find the cause of your confusion. When you have lifted up the son of man then shall you know that I AM he; that is, that I, John Smith, do nothing of myself but my father, or that state of consciousness which I am now one with does the works.

When this is realized every urge and desire that springs within you shall find expression in your world. "Behold I stand at the door and knock. If any man hear my voice and open the door I will come in to him and sup with him and he with me." The "I" knocking at the door is the urge.

The door is your consciousness. To open the door is to become one with that that which is knocking by FEELING oneself to be the thing desired. To feel one's desire as impossible is to shut the door or deny this urge expression.

To rise in consciousness to the naturalness of the thing felt is to swing wide the door and invite this one into embodiment. That is why it is constantly recorded that Jesus left the world of manifestation and ascended unto his father.

Jesus, as you and I, found all things impossible to Jesus, as man. But having discovered his father to be the state of consciousness of the thing desired, he but left behind him the

"Jesus consciousness" and rose in consciousness to that state desired and stood upon it until he became one with it. As he made himself one with that, he became that in expression.

This is Jesus' simple message to man: Men are but garments that the impersonal being "I AM", the presence that men call God, dwells in. Each garment has certain limitations. In order to transcend these limitations and give expression to that which as man, John Smith, you find yourself incapable of doing, you take your attention away from your present limitations — or John Smith conception of yourself — and merge yourself in the feeling of being that which you desire.

III

Just how this desire or newly attained consciousness will embody itself, no man knows. For "I AM", or the newly attained consciousness, has "ways that ye know not of"; its "ways are past finding out".

Do not speculate as to the HOW of this consciousness embodying itself, for no man is wise enough to know the how. Speculation is proof that you have not attained to the naturalness of being the thing desired and so are filled with doubts.

You are told, "He who lacks wisdom let him ask of God, that gives to all liberally, and upbraideth not; and it shall be given unto him. But let him ask not doubting for he who doubts is as a wave of the sea that is tossed and battered by the winds. And let not such a one think that he shall receive anything from the Lord." You can see why this statement is made, for only upon the rock of faith can anything be established.

If you have not the consciousness of the thing, you have not the cause or foundation upon which the thing is erected. A proof of this established consciousness is given you in the words, "Thank you, father." When you come into the joy of thanksgiving so that you actually feel grateful for having received that which is not yet apparent to the senses, you have definitely become one in consciousness with the thing for which you gave thanks.

God (your awareness) is not mocked. You are ever receiving that which you are aware of being and no man gives thanks for something which he has not received. "Thank you father" is not, as it is used by many today, a sort of magical formula. You need never utter aloud the words, "Thank you, father."

In applying this principle as you rise in consciousness to the point where you are really grateful and happy for having received the thing desired, you automatically rejoice and give thanks inwardly. You have already accepted the gift which was but a desire before you rose in consciousness, and your faith is now the substance that shall clothe your desire.

This rising in consciousness is the spiritual marriage where two shall agree upon being one, and their likeness or image is established on earth. "For whatsoever ye ask in my name the same give I unto you." 'Whatsoever' is quite a large measure. It is the unconditional. It does not state if society deems it right or wrong that you should ask it; it rests with you.

Do you really want it? Do you desire it? That is all that is necessary. Life will give it to you if you ask 'in his name.' His name is not a name that you pronounce with the lips. You can ask forever in the name of God or Jehovah or Christ Jesus and you will ask in vain. 'Name' means nature; so when you ask in the nature of a thing, results ever follow.

To ask in the name is to rise in consciousness and become one in nature with the thing desired. Rise in consciousness to the nature of the thing, and you will become that thing in expression.

Therefore, "what things soever ye desire, when ye pray, believe that ye receive them and ye shall receive them." Praying, as we have shown you before, is recognition – the injunction to "believe that ye receive" is first person, present tense. This means that you must be in the nature of the things asked for before you can receive them.

To get into the nature easily, general amnesty is necessary. We are told, "Forgive if ye have aught against any, that your father also, which is in Heaven, may forgive you. But if ye forgive not, neither will your father forgive you." This may seem to be some personal God who is pleased or displeased with your actions, but this is not the case.

Consciousness being God, if you hold in consciousness anything against man, you are binding that condition in your world. But to release man from all condemnation is to free yourself so that you may rise to any level necessary; there is therefore, no condemnation to those in Christ Jesus.

Therefore, a very good practice before you enter into your meditation is first to free every man in the world from blame. For LAW is never violated, and you can rest confidently in the knowledge that every man's conception of himself is going to be his reward. So you do not have to bother yourself about seeing whether or not man gets what you consider he should get. For life makes no mistakes and always gives man that which man first gives himself.

This brings us to that much abused statement of the Bible on tithing. Teachers of all kinds have enslaved man with this affair of tithing; for not themselves understanding the nature of tithing and being themselves fearful of lack, they have led their followers to believe that a tenth part of their income should be given to the Lord.

Meaning, as they make very clear, that, when one gives a tenth part of his income to their particular organization, he is giving his "tenth part" to the Lord (or is tithing). But remember, "I AM" the Lord." Your awareness of being is the God that you give to and that you ever give in this manner.

Therefore when you claim yourself to be anything, you have given that claim or quality to God. And your awareness of being, which is no respecter of persons, will return to you pressed down, shaken together, and running over with that quality or attribute which you claim for yourself.

Awareness of being is nothing that you could ever name. To claim God to be rich, to be great, to be love, to be all wise, is to define that which cannot be defined. For God is nothing that could ever be named.

Tithing is necessary and you do tithe with God. But from now on give to the only God, and see to it that you give him the quality that you desire as man to express by claiming yourself to be the great, the wealthy, the loving, the all wise.

Do not speculate as to how you shall express these qualities or claims, for life has a way that you as man know not of. Its ways are past finding out. But I assure you, the day you claim these qualities to the point of conviction, your claims will be honored.

There is nothing covered that shall not be uncovered. That which is spoken in secret shall be proclaimed from the housetops. That is, your secret convictions of yourself — these secret claims that no man knows of — when really believed, will be shouted from the housetops in your world. For your convictions of yourself are the words of the God within you, which words are spirit and cannot return unto you void but must accomplish where unto they are sent.

You are at this moment calling out of the infinite that which you are now conscious of being. And not one word or conviction will fail to find you.

"I AM the vine and ye are the branches." Consciousness is the 'vine,' and those qualities which you are now conscious of being are as 'branches' that you feed and keep alive. Just as a branch has no life except it be rooted in the vine, so likewise things have no life except you be conscious of them. Just as a branch withers and dies if the sap of the vine ceases to flow towards it, so do things in your world pass away if you take your attention from them; because your attention is as the sap of life that keeps alive and sustains the things of your world.

To dissolve a problem that now seems so real to you, all that you do is remove your attention from it. In spite of its seeming reality, turn from it in consciousness. Become indifferent, and begin to feel yourself to be that which would be the solution of the problem.

For instance, if you were imprisoned, no man would have to tell you that you should desire freedom. Freedom, or rather the desire of freedom, would be automatic. So why look behind the four walls of your prison bars? Take your attention from being imprisoned and begin to feel yourself to be free. FEEL it to the point where it is natural; the very second you do so, those prison bars will dissolve. Apply this same principle to any problem.

I have seen people who were in debt up to their ears apply this principle, and in the twinkling of an eye, debts that were mountainous were removed. I have seen those whom doctors had given up as incurable take their attention away from their problem of disease and begin to feel themselves to be well, in spite of the evidence of their sense to the contrary. In no time at all this so called "incurable disease" vanished and left no scar.

Your answer to "whom do you say that I AM?" ever determines your expression. As long as you are conscious of being imprisoned or diseased or poor, so long will you continue to out-picture or express these conditions. When man realizes that he is now that which he is seeking and begins to claim that he is, he will have the proof of his claim. This cue is given you in words, "Whom seek ye? And they answered, 'Jesus.'" And the voice said, "I am he." 'Jesus' here means salvation or savior. You are seeking to be salvaged from that which is not your problem.

"I am" is he that will save you. If you are hungry, your savior is food. If you are poor, your savior is riches. If you are imprisoned, your savior is freedom. If you are diseased, it will not be a man called Jesus who will save you, but health will become your savior. Therefore, claim "I am he". In other words, claim yourself to be the thing desired. Claim it in consciousness –

not in words – and consciousness will reward you with your claim. You are told, "You shall find me when you FEEL after me." Well, FEEL after that quality in consciousness until you FEEL yourself to be it.

When you lose yourself in the feeling of being it, the quality will embody itself in your world. You are healed from your problem when you touch the solution of it. "Who has touched me? For I perceive virtue is gone out of me." Yes, the day you touch this being within you — FEELING yourself to be cured or healed —virtues will come out of your very self and solidify themselves in your world as healings.

It is said, "You believe in God. Believe also in me for I am he." Have the faith of God. "He made himself one with God and found it not robbery to do the works of God." Go, you, and do likewise. Yes, begin to believe your awareness — your consciousness of being —to be God. Claim for yourself all the attributes that you have heretofore given an external God, and you will begin to express these claims.

"For I am not a God afar off. I am nearer than your hands and feet – nearer than your very breathing." I AM your awareness of being. I AM that in which all that I shall ever be aware of being shall begin and end. "For before the world was I AM; and when the world shall cease to be, I AM; before Abraham was, I AM." This I AM is your awareness.

"Except the Lord build the house they labor in vain that build it."— 'The Lord' being your consciousness; except that which you seek is first established in your consciousness, you will labor in vain to find it. All things must begin and end in consciousness.

So blessed indeed is the man that trusteth in himself, for man's faith in God will ever be measured by his confidence in himself. You believe in a God, believe also in ME.

Put not your trust in men for men but reflect the being that you are and can only bring to you or do unto you that which you have first done unto yourself.

"No man taketh away my life, I lay it down myself." I have the power to lay it down and the power to take it up again. No matter what happens to man in this world, it is never an accident. It occurs under the guidance of an exact and changeless Law.

"No man (manifestation) comes unto me except the father within me draw him," and "I and my father are one." Believe this truth and you will be free. Man has always blamed others for that which he is and will continue to do so until he find himself as cause of all.

"I AM" comes not to destroy but to fulfill. "I AM" — the awareness within you — destroys nothing but ever fill full the molds or conception one has of one's self.

It is impossible for the poor man to find wealth in this world no matter how he is surrounded with it until he first claims himself to be wealthy.

For signs follow, they do not precede. To constantly kick and complain against the limitations of poverty while remaining poor in consciousness is to play the fool's game. Changes cannot take place from that level of consciousness, for life is constantly out-picturing all levels.

Follow the example of the prodigal son. Realize that you yourself brought about this condition of waste and lack, and make the decision within yourself to rise to a higher level where the fatted calf, the ring, and the robe await your claim.

There was no condemnation of the prodigal when he had the courage to claim this inheritance as his own. Others will condemn us only as long as we continue in that for which we condemn ourselves. So, "Happy is the man that condemneth himself not in that which he alloweth." For to life nothing is condemned. All is expressed.

IV

Life does not care whether you call yourself rich or poor, strong or weak. It will eternally reward you with that which you claim as true of yourself. The measurements of right and wrong belong to man alone. To life there is nothing right or wrong.

As Paul stated in his letters to the Romans, "I know and am persuaded by the Lord Jesus that there is nothing unclean of itself, but to him that esteemeth anything to be unclean, to him it is unclean." Stop asking yourself whether you are worthy or unworthy to receive that which you desire. You, as man, did not create the desire. Your desires are ever fashioned within you because of what you now claim yourself to be.

When a man is hungry, without thinking, he automatically desires food. When imprisoned, he automatically desires freedom and so forth. Your desires contain within themselves the plan of self-expression. So leave all judgments out of the picture and rise in consciousness to the level of your desire and make yourself one with it by claiming it to be so now. For, "My grace is sufficient for thee. My strength is made perfect in weakness."

Have faith in this unseen claim until the conviction is born within you that it is so. Your confidence in this claim will pay great rewards. Just a little while and he, the thing desired, will come. But without faith it is impossible to realize anything. Through faith the worlds were framed because "faith is the substance of the thing hoped for, the evidence of the thing not yet seen."

Don't be anxious or concerned as to results. They will follow just as surely as day follows night. Look upon your desires — all of them — as the spoken words of God, and every word or desire a promise. The reason most of us fail to realize our desires is because we are constantly conditioning them. Do not condition your desire. Just accept it as it comes to you. Give thanks for it to the point that you are grateful for having already received it; then go about your way in peace.

Such acceptance of your desire is like dropping seed — fertile seed — into prepared soil. For when you can drop the thing desired in consciousness, confident that it shall appear, you have done all that is expected to you. But to be worried or concerned about the HOW of your desire maturing is to hold these fertile seeds in a mental grasp, and therefore, never to have dropped them in the soil of confidence.

The reason men condition their desires is because they constantly judge after the appearance of being and see the 'things' as real, forgetting that the only reality is the consciousness backing them. To see 'things' as real is to deny that all things are possible to God. The man who is imprisoned and sees his four walls as real is automatically denying the urge or promise of God within him of freedom.

A question often asked when this statement is made is: If one's desire is a gift of God, how can you say that if one desires to kill a man that such a desire is good and therefore God sent?

In answer to this let me say that no man desires to kill another. What he does desire is to be freed from such a one. But because he does not believe that the desire to be free from such a one contains within itself the powers of freedom, he conditions that desire and sees the only way to express such freedom is to destroy the man, forgetting that the life wrapped within the desire has ways that he, as man, knows not of. Its ways are past finding out.

Thus man distorts the gifts of God through his lack of faith. Problems are the mountains spoken of that can be removed if one has but the faith of a grain of a mustard seed. Men approach their problem as did the old lady who on attending service heard the priest say, "If you had but the faith of a grain of a mustard seed you would say unto yonder mountain 'be thou removed' and it shall be removed and nothing is impossible to you."

That night as she said her prayers, she quoted this part of the scriptures and retired to bed in what she thought was faith. On arising in the morning, she rushed to the window and exclaimed, "I knew that old mountain would still be there!"

For this is how man approaches his problem. He knows that they are still going to confront him. And because life is no respecter of persons and destroys nothing, it continues to keep alive that which he is conscious of being.

Things will disappear only as man changes in consciousness. Deny it if you will, it still remains a fact that consciousness is the only reality and things but mirror that which you are in consciousness. So the heavenly state you are seeking will be found only in consciousness, for the kingdom of heaven is within you. As the will of heaven is ever done on earth, you are today living in the heaven that you have established within you. For here on this very earth your heaven reveals itself. The kingdom of heaven really is at hand.

NOW is the accepted time. So create a new heaven, enter into a new state of consciousness, and a new earth will appear. "The former things shall pass away. They shall not be remembered, not come into mind anymore. For behold, I (your consciousness) come quickly and my reward is with me."

I AM nameless but will take upon myself every name (nature) that you call me. Remember it is you, yourself, that I speak of as 'me.' So every conception that you have of yourself — that is every deep conviction you have of yourself — is that which you shall appear as being, for I AM not fooled; God is not mocked.

Now let me instruct you in the art of fishing. It is recorded that the disciples fished all night and caught nothing. Then Jesus came upon the scene and told them to cast their nets in once more into the same waters that only a moment before were barren, and this time their nets were bursting with the catch.

This story is taking place in the world today right within you, the reader. For you have within you all the elements necessary to go fishing. But until you find that Jesus Christ (your awareness) is Lord, you will fish, as did these disciples, in the night of human darkness. That is, you will fish for THINGS, thinking 'things' to be real, and will fish with the human bait which is a struggle and an effort, trying to make contact with this one and that one, trying to coerce this being or the other being; and all such effort will be in vain. But when you discover your awareness of being to be Christ Jesus, you will let him direct your fishing. And you will fish in consciousness for the things that you desire. For your desire will be the fish that you will catch. Because your consciousness is the only living reality, you will fish in the deep waters of consciousness.

If you would catch that which is beyond your present capacity, you must launch out into deeper waters, for within your present consciousness such fish or desires cannot swim. To launch out into deeper waters, you leave behind you all that is now your present problem or limitation by taking your ATTENTION AWAY from it. Turn your back completely upon every problem and limitation that you now possess.

Dwell upon just being by saying, "I AM, I AM, I AM," to yourself. Continue to declare to yourself that you just are. Do not condition this declaration, just continue to FEEL yourself to be, and without warning you will find yourself slipping the anchor that tied you to the shallow of your problems and moving out into the deep.

This is usually accompanied with the feeling of expansion. You will FEEL yourself expand as though you were actually growing. Don't be afraid, for courage is necessary. You are not going to die to anything by your former limitations, but they are going to die as you move away from them, for they live only in your consciousness. In this deep or expanded consciousness, you will find yourself to be a power that you had never dreamt of before.

The things desired before you shoved off from the shores of limitation are the fish you are going to catch in this deep. Because you have lost all consciousness of your problems and barriers, it is now the easiest thing in the world to FEEL yourself to be one with the things desired.

Because I AM (your consciousness) is the resurrection and the life, you must attach this resurrecting power that you are to the thing desired, if you would make it appear and live in your world. Now you begin to assume the nature of the thing desired by feeling, "I AM wealthy", "I AM free", "I AM strong." When these 'FEELS' are fixed within yourself, your formless being will take upon itself the forms of the things felt.

You become 'crucified' upon the feelings of wealth, freedom, and strength. Remain buried in the stillness of these convictions. Then, as a thief in the night and when you least expect it, these qualities will be resurrected in your world as living realities. The world shall touch you and see that you are flesh and blood, for you shall begin to bear fruit of the nature of these qualities newly appropriated. This is the art of successful fishing for the manifestations of life.

Successful realization of the thing desired is also told us in the story of Daniel in the lion's den. Here it is recorded that Daniel, while in the lion's den, turned his back upon the lions and looked towards the light coming from above; that the lions remained powerless and Daniel's faith in his God saved him.

This also is your story, and you too must do as Daniel did. If you found yourself in a lion's den, you would have no other concern but lions. You would not be thinking of one thing in the world but your problem – which problem would be lions.

Yet, you are told that Daniel turned his back upon them and looked towards the light that was his God. If we would follow the example of Daniel we would, while imprisoned within the den of poverty of sickness, take our attention away from our problems of debts or sickness and dwell upon the thing we seek.

If we do not look back in consciousness to our problems but continue in faith, believing ourselves to be that which we seek, we too will find our prison walls open and the thing sought — yes, "whatsoever things" —realized.

Another story is told us of the widow and the three drops of oil. The prophet asked the widow, "What have ye in your house?" And she replied, "Three drops of oil." He then said to her, "Go borrow vessels. Close the door after ye have returned into your house and begin to pour." And she poured from three drops of oil into all the borrowed vessels, filling them to capacity with oil remaining.

You, the reader, are this widow. You have not a husband to impregnate you or make you fruitful, for a 'widow' is a barren state. Your awareness is now the Lord – or the prophet that has become your husband.

Follow the example of the widow, who instead of recognizing an emptiness or nothingness, recognized the something — three drops of oil. Then the command to her, "Go within and close the door." That is, shut the door of the senses that tell you of the empty measures, the debts, the problems.

When you have taken your attention away completely by shutting out the evidence of the senses, begin to FEEL the joy (symbolized by oil) of having received the things desired. When the agreement is established within you so that all doubts and fears have passed away, then you too will fill all the empty measures of your life and have an abundance running over.

Recognition is the power that conjures in the world. Every state that you have ever recognized, you have embodied. That which you are recognizing as true of yourself today is that which you are experiencing. So be as the widow and recognize joy, no matter how little the beginnings of recognition, and you will be generously rewarded. For the world is a magnified mirror, magnifying everything that you are conscious of being.

"I AM the Lord the God, which has brought thee out of the land of Egypt, out of the house of bondage; thou shalt have no other gods before me." What a glorious revelation, your awareness now revealed as the Lord thy God! Come, awake from your dream of being imprisoned. Realize that the earth is yours, "and the fullness thereof; the world, and all that dwells therein."

You have become so enmeshed in the belief that you are man that you have forgotten the glorious being that you are. Now with your memory restored, DECREE the unseen to appear and it SHALL appear, for all things are compelled to respond to the Voice of God — your awareness of being. The world is AT YOUR COMMAND!

www.ingramcontent.com/pod-product-compliance
Lightning Source LLC
LaVergne TN
LVHW041545070526
838199LV00046B/1836